Praise for Red Hawk's Poetry

***

This is such a strong book, written in a strong plain style. Red Hawk is like Whitman because he can contain multitudes and yet he is always so authentically himself. Behind all these [poems] there is always one single simple thing, which is Red Hawk's own voice. Haunting and stark, ironic and spare.

These poems are desperately important to us all today because Red Hawk has that rarest of all virtues (Virgil had it, Dante had it, Shakespeare had it)—a sense of civilization, something most of us have forgotten all about. Behind each of these miraculously crafted poems, Red Hawk speaks of the wise silence and the raw courage and the animal honesty and the elemental pride we will all be needing if we are to survive on this godforsaken planet as free men and women.

— The late William Packard
Editor, *New York Quarterly*

Other Books by Red Hawk

Poetry Collections:

Journey of the Medicine Man

The Sioux Dog Dance

The Way of Power

The Art of Dying

Wreckage With A Beating Heart

Raven's Paradise

Mother Guru

Return to the Mother

The Way of the Wise Woman

Nonfiction:

Self Observation: The Awakening of Conscience: An Owner's Manual

Self Remembering: The Path to Non-Judgmental Love: A Practitioner's Manual

The Law of the Land

Red Hawk

Aubade Publishing
Ashburn, VA

Copyright © 2020 Red Hawk

All rights reserved. No part of this publication may be reproduced, stored in a retrieval system, or transmitted in any form or by any means, electronic, mechanical, photocopying, recording, or otherwise, without the prior written permission of Aubade Publishing.

Edited by Joe Puckett

Cover and book design by Cosette Puckett

Cover photo by Gary Willets

Library of Congress Control Number: 2020930701

ISBN: 978-0-9845494-8-1

Published by Aubade Publishing, Ashburn, VA

Printed in the United States of America

Dedication: Sol Deo Gloria ("Glory to God Alone")

Yogi Ramsuratkumar: All Praise be Yours Beloved Father;
Mister Lee: Where can we go where You are not, Beloved Son;
Mister Gurdjieff: Teacher of Dancing;
Osho: Spiritual Warrior.

Chandrika: Dearest Worthy Companion—Unio Mystica;
Little Wind and Rain Drop: the moral force which wrought Essence-change.

Special thanks to the University of Arkansas at Monticello for the time off to finish this project, more than ten years in the making.

Note: Red Hawk is an Earth Name given by our Beloved Mother Earth as answered prayer after a 4-day water fast at the Buffalo River in the dead of winter, during one of the worst ice storms in recent Arkansas history. It is not an Indian name.

Contents

Prelude: The Law of the Land	2
I. The Requiem of Innocence: The Code of the Lakota	5
Words Are Not Actions	6
How the Lakota Tamed Their Wayward Sons	8
The Sweat Lodge	9
You and I Are Planting	10
The Arrowsmith Woman	11
The Seer's Counsel for the Buffalo Hunt	13
The Buffalo Dance	14
The Buffalo Hunt	15
Breaking the Heart of the Land	17
The Seer Offers Tobacco	18
The Camp Dogs	19
The Diet of Dogs	20
Apassionata: The Sioux Dog Dance	22
The Seer's Counsel to Young Warriors	24
The School of War	25
The Battle Axe	26
The Warrior's Spiritual Practice	27
The Seer's Counsel for Guarding the Horses	28
The Horses of War	29
He-Steals-Horses	31
Good Horse Nation	32
The Seer's Counsel for Surrender	34
The Position of Great Sacrifice	35
Sitting Bull Addresses the US Army Surrender Commission	37
Big Soldier Explains Why He Will Not Surrender	38
Hoka-Hey!	39
Elegy: What the Seer Foretold	41
Requiem: The Loss of Innocence	45
II. Earth Requiem: The Secret Teachings of the Forest	47
i. Stone	48
ii. River	49

Contents

iii. Tree	50
iv. Wolf	51
v. Wolf and Dog	52
vi. Dog	53
vii. Tree	54
viii. River	56
ix. Stone	57
x. Earth Requiem	58

III. The Requiem of Experience: The Indian Killer 61

The Indian Killer Interviewed	62
The Indian Killer and the Whore	64
The Indian Killer in Church	66
The Indian Killer's Father	68
The Indian Killer: Rules of Engagement	70
The Indian Killer Addresses the Question of Honor	72
The Indian Killer Explains Sharpshooting	74
The Indian Killer's Discourse on Art	75
The Indian Killer Joins Up with Cody	76
The Indian Killer Meets the President	78
The Indian Killer and Sitting Bull	80
The Indian Killer in Old Age	82

Dirge: Old Age Requires the Greatest Courage 83

The Indian Killer Speaks of Love	86
The Indian Killer Talks About Death	88
The Indian Killer's Vision	90
The Indian Killer on His Deathbed	92
Cody's Version of the Indian Killer	94
Sitting Bull Sees the Indian Killer	96
Elizabeth Joyce's Last Will & Testimony	98
President Franklin Pierce Is Questioned	100
The Preacher's Sworn Statement	101
The Indian Killer on Being Human	102

Requiem: The Indian Killer Explains Manifest Destiny 105

Postlude: Man and His Machines 107

But if you meditate
And follow the law
You will free yourself from desire

— Buddha, *Dhammapada*

Prelude:
The Law of the Land

The Law of the Land

The lay of the Land and
the play of the hand operate
under the same principle:
you play what is dealt you;

it shapes your life by what is given
and what is taken away.
The voice of the Land is in the Crow
and the wind in the tree,

in the creek and the tumbled stone
which is shaped by the shifting currents,
the torrent and the dwindling trickle.
What is removed, worn down,

worn away, leaves what is left,
what is necessary, that which
nothing need be added to nor
taken from.

The Land grinds fine, boulder
to pebble, then to grain of sand, then
to dust blown by the wind.
The Land gives, it takes away;

you may fight or yield, plow
or allow the field to lie fallow,
cut your own path or follow
the watercourse way; it is all the same.

First the Land will tame you,
then it will claim what belongs to it.
The fool believes he owns the Land;
the Wise man knows he is owned, and

all that he has is loaned.

I. The Requiem of Innocence:
The Code of the Lakota

Quietly consider
What is right and what is wrong.
Receiving all opinions equally,
Without haste, wisely,
Observe the law

— Buddha, *Dhammapada*

"Those sorcerers called this ability to perceive energy as it flowed in the universe *seeing*," Don Juan explained to me. "They described *seeing* as a state of heightened awareness in which the human body is capable of perceiving energy as a flow, a current, a windlike vibration. To *see* energy as it flows in the universe is the product of a momentary halt of the system of interpretation proper to human beings"

— Don Juan Matus to Carlos Castaneda, *Magical Passes*

Seeing happens only when one is capable of shutting off the internal dialogue

— Carlos Castaneda, *Tales of Power*

Words Are Not Actions

The Lakota followed the Great Law:
Pay Attention.
Go Slow.
Be Still.

A man stood by his word, or
he could not live among the people.
This was how the Whites were different;
among them, words were cheap.

The Lakota knew better.
Before a warrior went into battle
he did not speak. In the Sweat Lodge
he drummed and sang and prayed,

then spent 3 days in solitude
preparing his Heart for his death.
When he was ready to ride, his woman
handed him axe and bow.

Their gaze met and held.

No word was spoken.
Some came back dead or badly wounded.
There was a big fire; all gathered
to hear the tales of battle.

The warriors laughed and laughed,
made jokes about each other.
They knew the wounds would heal,
knew the dead would be fed to the birds.

The Lakota had a saying:
Words fall down on the ground
like shit from the dogs;
deeds lift a man up

like the Spirit leaving the body.

How the Lakota Tamed Their Wayward Sons

Each spring at gelding time,
the Lakota men
gathered all of the bad boys,
those whose sap was at the boil
and overflowing without control

and they took them among the horses,
sorting out those who did not respond
to proper training,
to be gelded.
They held the horse and yelled at it,
You will not do as you are told!
and then strong men held them down

while the task of two bad boys was
to take wet rawhide and loop it
around the horse's balls,
drawing it tight as another boy
cut and sliced
with a sharp knife or finely honed
clam shell from the Great Lakes.

At the end of this ritual, the men
roasted their spoils and
ate them with relish, offering some
to the young boys who would
often refrain.
The Lakota
never had any trouble
with their sons.

The Sweat Lodge

The Sweat Lodge is the theater of the absurd;
you go in with your act intact,
a well-fortified strategy which you call
a self. Then the stones and heat
and sweat and suffering go to work,
expose the self as lies and frail conceits,
strip it all down
to the absurd.

This self cannot save you with its lying
in moments of profound distress,
despite everything you've heard;
under extreme duress
it breaks down in the heat
and makes a crying sound
like a hurt animal dying,
not like any spoken human word.

Once you are broken, something
emerges without the lying
or the mind's illusion of self;
it is stable and still, unmoved
when an ill-wind blows, able
to till the soil of the Heart
and make it yield a Soul, from fire
and a field of hurt desire.

You and I Are Planting

The Lakota, whose language
was as simple as their life,
did not have a single word
called Love the way we do.
They had instead a phrase,

You and I are planting,

and it meant something like
what we would call Love, only
it was not the same. It meant
what it says,
planting. It implies

a seed in fertile soil,
moisture, light, patience,
good luck and above all
Grace from praying and
from careful tending of the Land;

caretakers, not creators,
servants in a kindly labor.
This is a humble way with words;
like placing seeds in a hole
made with a sharp stick, it does not

isolate them from the Land
upon which their life depends.
One pokes, one plants.
Together they weed,
they pluck the bloom.

The Arrowsmith Woman

Her work is wood and feather.
She holds the branch softly in her hand,
straight Hickory branch, cuts it thankfully
and with a prayerful regret, the way
a woman cuts the cord
to set her baby free.

She fire-hardens, strips it,
shaves it round and round until
the balance is perfectly right;
like 2 lovers who live apart, the art
is to find the exact midpoint between
longing and lingering.

She traps small birds by patience and luck
to take them alive, then carefully plucks
3 feathers, the number required for an arrow,
then releases them unharmed, Jay, Sparrow,
Warbler, Dove. The hunters trust her skill, her love,
her stillness when shaping the feathers so

they fly true in the Heart of the wood.
She cradles them like lifting a newborn
to her breast, notching, paring, fitting, gluing
with minute attention to detail, sparing
no effort; the cultivation of Attention
shapes her inner life, is her secret reward.

The hunters hold her in high regard and she
hands her life's work over to them, the way a woman
gives her child to the world in delicate consent,
having done all things possible to make it
true to its aim, able to give beautifully
and to take terribly away.

In her hands she held the people's fate;
everything depended on the hunters shooting straight.

The Seer's Counsel for the Buffalo Hunt

You bless the spearpoint with your own blood:
all blood is the same Heart of the World, so once
the point tastes blood, it goes straight for the Heart.

You pray for your prey:
that they may give themselves so that you
will live, you bow down in gratitude.

You study their every move:
all mammals repeat their habits, therefore
you know where to wait and when to strike.

Never take more than is necessary:
to give in to desire
is to become the hunted.

Aim with clear Intention:
when the Buffalo is in your sights,
do not hesitate or he will turn on you

and you are lost.

The Buffalo Dance

We are a nation junked on speed, but

George Catlin, the painter of Indians,
tells of a different mentality,
of a native race rooted in the dirt,
people who knew how to wait.

Once he was privileged to stay with the Lakota,
a Plains nation whose survival depended upon
their relationship with the Buffalo.
When he arrived, they were beginning

the Buffalo Dance,
hunters in paint and feathers, spears
beaded and feathered, rattles and drums.
In the middle was a lone dancer, covered

with a Buffalo robe who, over and over,
advanced, was killed, and died slowly.
This went on for days and days and
then more days until finally Catlin grew

bored and impatient. He could not imagine
dancing night and day like this. How long
does this go on? he asked. They looked at him
as if he were crazy.

Until the Buffalo come, they replied.

The Buffalo Hunt

Nothing else mattered half so much
as the Buffalo hunt; everything
depended on it.

For the Lakota hunters
life was in the chase;
everything else was just waiting.

Even battle took a back saddle
to riding up on 1500 pounds
of pure muscle and

leaning out over the hump at full speed,
holding onto the pony only with your thighs
so you could get a full draw with the bow

and place the arrow in the soft spot
forward of the hump and just
between the shoulders,

exactly there   and
the great machinery stumbled   and
fell and

the way of life, the Spirit of the people,
unrolled and played out to the last dark day
from   that   shot   and

once the Buffalo began to disappear
then the end drew near, was in plain sight;
the only thing left to them was a hopeless fight

with no logic in it save the choosing
to die with courage, while losing
everything but Honor; only that remained

when Mercy disappeared from the world.

Breaking the Heart of the Land

For the Lakota Sioux
the slaughter of the Buffalo was
catastrophic.

It is not written in the histories, but
the distant echo, the fading drumming
of 6 million hoofbeats
carried away on the prairie wind,
was a lamentation, a dirge,
a devastating loneliness

which haunted the Land when the ghosts
of the Buffalo passed that way and
then vanished,

exposing a darkness in the heart of Mankind.
The Lakota were destroyed.
Some truths take a long time to manifest,
but the loss of the Buffalo broke the hearts
of the Lakota all at once, and forever.
And it broke the Heart of the Land.

But the Land endured the violation of its Heart:
the seed-bearing trees brought forth their
    succulent fruits,
the creeping plants gave up their tender shoots,
and the tubers and dirt-swelled edibles offered
    their roots;
each soil-worshipping species clothed in dirt
offered up its prayers to heal the hurt.

The Seer Offers Tobacco

Whoever comes to him, it does not matter
whether enemy or friend, he makes the offer
of tobacco and they smoke the pipe;
whether it means war or the hope

of peace is not his main prayer,
nor is such a thing in his power.
He offers what the Earth has given
in Her bounty; as it is in heaven,

so it is here: not by his will alone,
but by the Grace of the Holy Unknown,
all things come to their rightful end;
he takes what is his from the Land

and gives it into his body as sacrament,
Blessing friend and foe alike. He is the instrument
of Grace and lives by the Law of Hospitality,
welcoming all without hostility

or thought of personal gain.
If he kills you or dies by your hand,
he has made the noble gesture
and prepares to die in the right posture:

he passes the pipe and bows to his death;
he lives in the silent pause between each breath.

The Camp Dogs

They ran wild, hunted down their own prey, so
they were no drain on the common stores and
they raised the alarm when there was

a raiding party, someone come to steal the horses,
or a war party on foot over the ridge.
It gave the warriors time to gather their forces

and get in position on a ledge
overlooking the enemy, then wipe them out.
The dogs had loyalties, came on a shout

or a whistle from the ones they loved;
when the Lakota did the Dog Dance
after their surrender, it was partly to honor

the dog's loyalty, the time before the reservation
when the dogs kept them warm at night and
when all else failed, kept them from starvation.

The Diet of Dogs

The Indians ate their dogs only when
they had to, and not with relish, but
with regret and Sacred ceremony,
because that last hard winter,
as the white terror moved across the land,

the dogs were all that stood between them
and starvation.
While the terrorists talked about salvation
and the god that loved them,
they ate their dogs.

Life becomes absurd when you are
forced to eat your dogs; then
you learn that impossible
is an arbitrary line
drawn in the snow and

the first strong wind
blows it away,
leaving you with nothing
but the last dog and
no end to the cold wind.

Apassionata:
The Sioux Dog Dance

The Sioux Dog Dance

They came from Washington by special train,
generals, senators, their wives and mistresses
to see how the reservation had civilized the Sioux.

The Sioux made a new dance for the occasion.

The day was so hot flies died in the dust
but the rich and powerful were there
in the fort's reviewing stand   talking

when the big drum started on the parade ground.
They were pleased by the wooden cross they spied
in the center of the field. Then the 2 leaders came,

the Medicine Man and his woman, dancing naked,
holding up 2 howling dogs by their hind legs tied;
by their hind legs they hung them from the cross.

All talking ceased at once.

From her hair she pulled a knife and in one sweep
sliced the first dog from tail to tongue, then
passed the knife; he did the same.

Some women fainted; all were frozen, wide-eyed.
She pulled and sliced the organs into strips;
each took one in their teeth, then

2 lines of naked dancers spun onto the field,
one by one approached the leaders, with their teeth
received the strips, swung them side to side

until they all had taken and the blood dried
on their faces. Then they ate them.
On the stand there was no place to hide.

No one moved.
The drums went silent, the dancers cried
Aiieee Yiiip!

and the black flies buzzed there as they died.

The Seer's Counsel to Young Warriors

For the Lakota there were no
meaningless acts, no wasted gestures,
the form of one's actions
was just as important as the content,
and form required vigilance and
totality of Intention,
nothing withheld.

The Seer's advice
was sought
by young warriors ready to pay the price,
preparing to die before they fought:

*Life is a great river
that takes us all to the Shining Waters;
we are all born to die so
everything matters;
while you have life, savor
every breath;
fortune favors
those who give their entire Spirit to the endeavor
so hold nothing back in all your labors.
It is never over.
Prepare each day for your death
and if you are going to die in battle, never*

die with arrows in your quiver.

The School of War

War defines one of many edges of a man;
the line between cruelty and compassion
is rendered in varying shades of blood.

The Seer said of war,
*It is the moment when a man's life
turns from flesh into a red mist and*

*if he emerges still dressed as a human being
his eyes have grown dark with the loss
of his eagerness,*

*he is silenced by what he has endured,
humbled by seeing what he is capable of;
only then is every breath sacred.*

The Lakota schooled their sons in war
so they could endure the peace.
Having killed, they could withstand privation

without complaint, being wounded
they could tolerate pain, and
having lost everything, death

held neither enticement nor mystery:
it could no longer seduce or placate,
only gesture, whisper, entreat, and implore;

the warrior stood indifferent to its charms.

The Battle Axe

As soon as the boy was born, the men
went into the woods and selected
a Hickory tree, carrying a heavy
worked stone.

They split one strong green limb and
drove wedges into it carefully until
it was wide enough to take the stone.
Then they left it.

In his 13th summer he came with the men
to cut the limb at the trunk. The stone
was part of the tree, immovable,
heavy as thunder.

This was his axe.
He had to grow into it; it required
more muscle to wield with the
necessary grace to kill a man.

It taught him patience, when to give
and how to take away; it taught him
respect for the tool and
for the job it was made to do.

The Warrior's Spiritual Practice

When Sitting Bull was a young boy,
each boy was given a small bow
and a quiver of arrows.
They had many games which sharpened
their ability with the bow.

When the other boys grew bored,
Sitting Bull continued to practice
endlessly, never tiring of finding
more and more elusive targets, until
it was said he grew so skilled
that he could hit grasshoppers and
dragonflies on the fly.

When asked by the other boys
why he spent so much time
honing this skill, he said,

When I am not practicing,
somewhere, someone is practicing
to perfect his aim, and

when we meet
he will kill me, so
I never stop.

The Seer's Counsel for Guarding the Horses

Be ever vigilant in the guarding of the herd:
the horses are always restless and subject
to every small distraction; do not sleep.

No sudden moves:
the horses are easily spooked and will
kick one another to death if frightened.

Observe even the slightest movement:
the thieves are subtle and move with great
delicacy, but each movement is your advantage.

Do not fight openly when under attack:
if you move silently and invisibly
among the startled herd, you will not be taken.

Do not lose yourself in the midst of chaos:
always know who you are and where you are
even when thieves come in the dead of night.

The vigilant guard lives to see the dawn.

The Horses of War

You can hear the clink, chink, clank
of their armor a long time before you
see them, the glint from the Sun

nearly blinding you as they ride
steady and slow in formation
across the shallowest part of the river,

their hooves light and eager to charge.
This is before they have seen their blood
spilled by a lance piercing their flank

so they are brought down and struggle
to rise, before they are riderless and
stampeded in the mayhem of screams and

trample the dead and dying in their dash
to the trees. Now they are head high,
big yellow teeth set on the iron bit,

bridle streaming with feathers,
paint on their withers. They are
full of themselves, as the air

will be thick and full of arrows,
a hundred wounds drawing rivers of blood
until the water runs red and

the screams of horses and men
raise a symphony,
a choir of weeping

from which the angels
cover their ears and
turn their faces away.

He-Steals-Horses

He once brought back 21 ponies
in a single foray; no one did it better.
When you stay with a thing long enough

a doorway opens for you
into another dimension;
that's when the real magic happens.

The body's wiring gets rearranged.
This is the secret
of giving your life to a practice

like stealing horses.
There came a moment for him when
it was no longer about the horses,

it was about the art of becoming invisible,
disappearing so completely that
the sentries who guarded the horses

never caught a glimpse of him and
the dogs never sniffed his scent on the air.
That is when the whispering began and

his feats of daring became legendary.
When you stay with a thing long enough,
it reveals such beauty that

even his enemies honor the thief,
bow down in disbelief,
and the Heart breaks, despite itself.

Good Horse Nation
(Oyate Shunkawakan Waste)

The white terrorists brought their diseases
which spread across the land like a dense rising flood
in the blood where there was no defense;
not shield nor axe, bow nor lance
can stop the slaughter; it takes what it pleases

and

they also brought horses, sleek
lean muscular rangy mustangs
with speed and great endurance.
The Lakota took to them
the way a fledgling takes to air
and they proved to be insurance

against hunger and tribal warfare.
The Lakota became a horse nation,
human and horse bonded in a love affair
broken only by the great white terror.
At full gallop, man, horse, arrow and bow
were enough to take down the Buffalo.

Navigating an ocean of Prairie grass by starlight,
miles from shore, grass moving in waves of wind,
across it comes a tidal wave faster
than the fleetest pony, uprooting everything,
Buffalo and horse and Lakota,

it took them all down like a little town
made of sticks and mud on the oceanside
inundated by the relentless rising tide,
nowhere to run, nowhere to hide.

The Seer's Counsel for Surrender

Be still:
guard your tongue lest it betray you,
be aware that your words can slay you.

Don't give them reason to shoot you:
stay low, lay down, be invisible as a root,
they don't shoot what they can't see.

Don't believe a word they say:
they lie as a way of life and their lies
will cut out your heart like a knife.

Wait patiently for your time to come:
all things come around in their season;
one day they will be cut down for no reason.

Accept what you cannot change:
be fluid as the mountain stream flows,
follow wherever the spring wind blows

and live to once again hunt the Buffalo.

The Position of Great Sacrifice

It was Sitting Bull they turned to when
all about them was in ruins,
their lodges burned and the Buffalo
wiped out from the plains.

It was the Chief who rallied the young men
when the old ones had exhausted their force;
he rode among them on his warhorse
and shook his axe in their faces.

Though he knew the fight was lost, he
understood the cost of yielding to the Whites
without a fight to the death, and so
with axe and shield in hand

he rode with them into the valley of death.
And it was given to his breath alone,
when women and children starved and froze,
to make the surrender speech in his finest clothes

and hand the Eagle feather in his hair
to hollow men who did not know nor care
what any of it meant; they made an empty show
of promises that he knew no ear would hear

nor tongue would ever honor.
Then he prayed to Crow and Deer
to follow the people in their sorrow and shame:
Deer to provide them with game,

Crow to pick clean the bones of those who fell,
and to leave one true voice left to tell
what it means to speak the truth in hell.
A man must do the job he is given.

Sitting Bull Addresses the US Army Surrender Commission (September 1874)

The Buffalo are gone,
wiped out.
That is the end of us, so
now we are made to surrender.
I do not know what surrender means.
Did the Buffalo surrender?
It seems that is what is meant
by surrender.
I have never surrendered before so
I look to the buffalo for an answer;
the Buffalo tell me,
to surrender is to be wiped out,
to disappear from the Earth forever.
Now you ask me to disappear
along with the Buffalo and
I am glad to do it.
Without the Buffalo we are nothing.
One day you will be asked to surrender;
on that day Sitting Bull will be standing
by the Buffalo waiting to greet you, not
looking down from your heaven but
looking up from our Earth.
Do what you want with Sitting Bull,
he knows where his feet are, he knows
where he stands.

Big Soldier Explains Why He Will Not Surrender

He was one of the Battle Chiefs of the Lakota and he
would not surrender, though he urged his people to
because he saw they were starving and finished;
when a colonel at Fort Phil Kearney questioned him

about why he would not lay down his arms
it is reported that Big Soldier replied,
*I see you admire your manner of living;
you can do almost what you choose.*

*You whites possess the power of subduing
almost every animal to your use;
you are surrounded
by slaves.*

*Everything about you is in chains
and you are slaves yourselves.
I fear that if I should exchange
my pursuits for yours*

*I would forget who I am, live indoors,
and cease being brave;
I too should become a slave
and the People would spit on Big Soldier's grave.*

Hoka-Hey!

The Lakota knew when to run,
when to stand and fight;
they were not afraid to die.

Every morning the parents
took their children to the door of the lodge
and greeted the Sun with tobacco or corn

cast before the doorway; they said,
Hoka-Hey! which means *It's a good day to die!*
They acquainted their children with death.

This gave them their edge in battle,
their courage to risk death, because
they knew they came from the Earth

and were honored and joyful
to return to Her; but more importantly
this gave them their edge in life because

they were slow to anger, quick to forgive
knowing this was the day, this very day,
that they would die.

When a man faces death in this way
he makes for good company; he is
always ready to smoke the pipe and

eager to laugh and make a joke.
He would not be one who spoke
badly of others, or too long, or

too often.

Elegy:
What the Seer Foretold

What the Seer Foretold

He was old before any of the warriors were grown
and when they were young they feared him,
would run away so as not to be caught alone
with him. He was all wrinkle, glare and bone
and the old ones in the tribe revered him,
but the young ones wouldn't go near him.

One night the whole tribe gathered around a fire;
the Seer threw bones in the dirt,
poured water over hot stones, made a cloud
of steam that rose around him higher
than the lodge poles, and he said the Hurt
was coming thick as this white cloud, a loud

thunder over the plains like 100 Buffalo herds
would drown out the cries of the people, and
only the dead would ever hear their words;
a hard fire would sweep over the land
and wipe out the Lakota, all brave men would die,
and white-faced ghosts who could only tell a lie

would steal the Lakota land and kill all the Buffalo.
The young bucks hooted at him in scorn,
said he was old and had lost his head
while the old ones hung their heads in sorrow.
Too soon, most of the young men were dead
and those left alive cursed the day they were born.

The old people knew
when the Seer speaks
the fish stop to listen in the creeks,
the snakes crawl closer in the tall grasses
and trees still the wind as it passes.

The old Seer always knows
which way the cold wind blows.

＃ *Requiem:*
The Loss of Innocence

The Loss of Innocence

Perhaps you've heard the wind come through the leaves
like a child's fingers rustling paper, and
how just afterwards everything goes still
and even in the warmest air a subtle chill
moves momentarily across the land,
as if there were a loss, and something grieves

for what it once had and cannot retrieve.
There is an ancient memory in the land
which moves unseen through dust and dirt and stone
the way it does through blood and flesh and bone.
What has been lost we can barely understand:
we cast aside our love of Earth like scattered leaves.

The land itself is filled with deep remorse,
the way the heart is broken by divorce.

II. Earth Requiem:
The Secret Teachings of the Forest

You go against the law,
You go into the dark.
Your pleasures end in fear

— Buddha, *Dhammapada*

Only if one loves this earth with unbending passion can one release one's sadness. A warrior is always joyful because his love is unalterable and his beloved, the earth, bestows upon him inconceivable gifts . . . . Only the love for this splendorous being can give freedom to a warrior's spirit; and freedom is joy, efficiency, and abandon in the face of any odds

— Don Juan Matus to Carlos Castaneda, *Tales of Power*

Be at one with the dust of the earth.
This is primal union

— Lao Tsu, *Tao Te Ching*

i. Stone

Be patient.

A huge stone may wait 10,000 years without a quiver
until exactly the right moment
when it tumbles down the mountain
in an ecstasy of movement,
hurling itself into the river;
for 1,000 years more
it may stand as a monument of will,
resisting the river's roar,
its fierce tear and relentless wear, until

exactly the right opportunity,
at the peak of the thousandth springtime flood,
it begins its slow deliberate pilgrimage.
Down stony bed, through swirl of mud
and floating log, over ancient Cedar root
it crushes its way in countless eons to the sea.

No desiring.

The ancient Seer comes to the swollen river,
lays his body beneath his ally, old Cedar tree,
gazes in wonder at the huge stone surging
just under the surface of the urgent flood.
Without desire, calm and steady in his gaze,
he prepares to retire from his flesh and blood.

There is no need for desire.

ii. River

Be fluid.

The river flows cleanly through the trees,
always downhill, always seeking ease
of movement, the path of least resistance:
say a huge stone is hurled in its path
and for a thousand years
through melt and swell of winter storm
or burst of springtime flood,
it scarcely budges.

The river adjusts,
goes along, goes around,
has no fight with anything,
just yields ground;
it barely nudges,
parries instead of thrusts.
Slowly, the river brings
tall mountains down.

No resisting.

By the swollen torrent, that same Seer,
old in his days and ways, riven
with the sorrows of the flesh and given
to Visions, sheds the rags of his past
and lies down naked in his dying, at last
freed of decisions, freed of tomorrows
and the cares of the body, freed of the torment
of loss, he seeks the last dark Vision.

There is no need to resist.

iii. Tree

Be rooted.

200 years on a gentle grassy rise,
deep-rooted Cedar guards the river;
it is undressed by winter.
Its high branches root the sky.
The Seer made it his ally.
He comes now, lies down for his final rest.
When young, he took refuge beneath this tree,
a place of comfort and well-being
where he learned the art of Seeing
and was given the Visions
to guide the people in their decisions;
now it would set him free.
He learned that a man is wise
who follows his heart and does not waver;
when rooted in Attention, he is blessed.

No drifting.

He has come to his tree to die,
to feed the body to his ally.
His mind wants to drift
but he is strong in his heart,
has earned the gift
of Attention. By fit and start
body gives in to surprise of death; he lifts
up through high branches, tumbles into the sky.

There is no need to drift.

iv. Wolf

Be watchful.

She never had a chance;
she was hit without warning
as she loped easily down the river trail,
nose up to take the man-scent
she had smelled for miles. She never saw
the trap hidden in the deep snow
and it snapped her paw with relish
in its massive metal jaw.

No wavering.

Without hesitation she began to chew her way free.
Like a dark cloud staining a summer sky,
blood spread in the snow; she made no cry.
Within minutes tendon and bone gave way
and she began her slow crawl to safety,
dragging the bloody stump a few feet,
stopping to lick, rising again weakly.

In this way she went a mile toward her den
before she found the body by the river,
under the Cedar tree where it lay concealed.
She fed on it until she healed.
On 3 legs she scavenged then.

Now she watches, never running;
she follows her nose with unwavering intent.
Once she was a swift killing instrument;
now she is all patient nostril cunning.

There is no need to waver.

v. Wolf and Dog

Be free.

The winter was bitter and hard so
she was starving as she struggled
on 3 legs down the river trail.

Naturally, she was surprised to see
the dog appear, so fat
and sleek of fur.

In her own way, she asked the dog
his circumstances,
how he came by his meat.

In his own way, the dog
begged the wolf to come to his home
and the wolf, who was starving, agreed.

No dependence.

When they neared the edge of the forest
she spotted the collar on the dog's neck
and in her own way asked about it.

She learned then about the men who own beasts;
she stopped; in the spring, under the giant Cedar,
they found her body by the river, starved.

There is no need to be dependent.

vi. Dog

Pay Attention.

He watched and watched for more than a year
as the Humans came and went, unlatched the gate,
until a light shone through his veil of fear
and he saw the chance to control his own fate.
With paw and teeth and then his nose
he worked to lift the latch and slide it roughly
from its sheath, then pushed and he was free.

No distraction.

He worked his way down the alley in back,
at each gate with a dog he unlatched and pushed.
Some stood dumbly, unmoving, spirits too far crushed
to see; but a few at once rushed to form a pack.
He led them to the forest, to the giant Cedar tree,
where her scent still lingered, and they ran
until they found the hidden cave where she had lived.
One by one, they chewed each other's collar through,
then were free to live and die as wild things do.

There is no need to be distracted.

vii. Tree

Man belongs to the Earth.

The first men who came worshipped the tree;
they called it Grandfather.
The only tools they had were made of wood and stone
and the power came from their bodies alone:
one man, with one tool, in one day;
in this way
they measured time;
they respected their place,
worked at their body's pace,
remained in harmony with the land, aligned.

The first cut:
then came the long saw, one man on each end;
they took down the forest, chained the logs,
hooked them to horses, dragged them
to the river, floated them downstream.
When they had the power to do more
than their bodies alone could manage,
they took more than was their need,
forgot what they were here for,
and entered into a bad dream.
This was the beginning of the age of greed.
The tree endured.

No greed.

The second cut:
machines replaced men and men forgot
both their limits and their place;
their allegiance shifted and with it
their worship of the land was lost;
they confused value with cost.
The forest dwindled, then as some men feared,
the forest disappeared.
When the giant Cedar blocked the great dam project,
like a virus they took it down with their power:
one machine, in less than an hour.

There is no need for greed.

viii. River

For every thing there is a season.

The first men who came worshipped the river;
it was *a strong brown god;*
they called It Grandmother
and they travelled It in awe and wonder,

in small canoes made from the bark of trees,
one man, under his own power, at the mercy
of the river's whim; it brought them to their knees.

They built small, mobile villages in places
the river spared in its flooding. They left few traces
when they moved. They studied the flow,
knew where to build and when to go.

No life without the flow.

First village, then town, then city
built on a flood plain, wiped out
now and then by the river.

The age of the great dam came.
Many men with huge machines
built a grand dam to tame

and control the river.
Then they drank the river up
until it could not reach the sea.
They worshipped the dam as a deity.

There is no need to lose the flow.

ix. Stone

The Earth remains.

Stone has a beauty of its own:
mass, density, and weight,
immensity of Presence
and intensity of place,
position
and the absence of desire;
what moves a stone
is not its will alone,
but the will of something higher.

No desire.

A round river stone held in the hand
soothes the troubled mind,
while a boulder anchors the land,
oversees it though it is blind.
All men are comforted by stone;
we know it will stand in a fierce storm
and in its Presence we do not feel alone;
we sense that we will come to no harm.

The beauty of a stone is its patient grace;
having had enough of the fast flood's pace,
it stops. It stays in place.
Mankind arose and vanished; its time was brief
because it crept in the night like a thief
and stole all it was given, so it came to grief.
When even the river was drained,
the stone alone remained.

There is no need for desire.

x. Earth Requiem

Only good will come of this.

In time, the forest roots begin to sprout;
the pools that remain in riverbeds hold trout
and the fire that consumed all, burns out.
Once the humans flee
the animals return, gratefully;
some nest in the green tree
which is tender of limb and leaf, not steady
yet in the wind, thrown about by rain
and bent double like an old man in pain.
Still it rightens like a ship in a storm-tossed sea
and the Earth knows, in its organic memory,
how to regain the Sacred, delicate harmony:
The Gospel according to the stones;
the Book of Trees; the Psalms of the River god.

No despair.

The wind is its breath,
the rain its rhythmic singing;
in one hand
it holds death,
in the other the flocked birds winging,
and a stillness comes over the land.
All things pass away, bringing
rich rot to the fertile forest soil. No grief
attends to the season of the fallen leaf,
no mourning the death of the 2-legged thief

lost in an old dark shadow: the deeper the debt
the steeper the payment; the land does not forget,
it always collects what is owed,
first slowly, then all at once the world implodes.

There is no need for despair.

III. The Requiem of Experience:
The Indian Killer

*Read as few words as you like
And speak fewer.
But act upon the law*

— Buddha, *Dhammapada*

"Thus to be a warrior a man has to be, first of all, and rightfully so, keenly aware of his own death.... So the next thing one needs to be a warrior is detachment. The idea of imminent death, instead of becoming an obsession, becomes an indifference. Detach yourself from everything"

— Carlos Castaneda, *A Separate Reality*

*If men are not afraid to die,
It is of no avail to threaten them with death.
If men live in constant fear of dying,
And if breaking the law means that a man will be killed,
Who will dare to break the law?*

— Lao Tsu, *Tao Te Ching*

The Indian Killer Interviewed

I killed hundreds, warriors, women and children.
Any regrets? he is asked.
Not a one about that; I done my duty, he sighs.
They's all Injuns; never killed a white man
on purpose.

The only good Injun is a dead one.
He laughs. I'm the one first said that,
but lots took credit for it. Truth is,
the truth is shifty, hard to draw a bead on it;
you think ya gotta good shot lined up,
then you see ya missed by a mile.

His one good eye squints; the other
was lost by knife in a bar fight.
There's just 3 things I regret, he says:
first there's nobody left to fight;
second my boy takes after me, real hellion.
The devil that's in you don't look half bad until
he shows up in yr child, he says.

Then you see what took yr heart.
What took yours? he is asked.
He lets it sit there for a minute.
The killin', he finally says.
Once a dog kills a chicken,
you got to shoot it, 'cuz he'll never stop;
sometimes I think he's got all the luck,
the dog that gets shot.

Then there was this whore, he says and
his good eye shines like a bright Moon
in a dark sky. I got nothin' left or
left to lose. Losin' her,
all the good went outta the world.

The Indian Killer and the Whore

She was a bar whore, wasn't much to look at but
she was good to me, who was never good for nothin'
nor good to nobody. When I got cut bad in a bar fight,
gut stabbed, lost one eye, she took me in, nursed me
for weeks until I healed. That was the first time;
the other time I got the fever and shakes
from a Chinese whore. She never makes me talk,
don't say nothin', just takes me in and
nurses me 'til I was well.
I liked to die, wasn't for her I wd of.

We had the boy, poor lad.
He grew up in a whore house. I done
lousy by him, never stayed one place long enough.
He follered after me every time I left, hollerin',
then he quit. That hurt me.
I knew I wasn't no good, but
I wanted better for him. She was
a good mother but she spoiled him and
I was too hard boiled, so a good lad
went bad.

When they told me she had 2 weeks to live, I give
up the Army, went back and stayed with her, prayed
first, then cursed God. I seen a lotta bad, but the worst
was watchin' her die hard, cryin' out, tryin' to
hold on to me, growin' cold, beggin' me to shoot her.
She was the only one I wdn't shoot,
cdn't. Lotsa others begged me not to,

but the only one ever begged me to,
I cdn't do it. I don't feel half so bad about
all them I killed as I do about the one
I cdn't.

The Indian Killer in Church

Did you ever attend church? he is asked.
He gives a throaty growl, half laugh,
half curled-lip howl.
Twice the whore took me with the lad,
he says. There's one for ya,
a church-goin whore, but
that's how she was. So I went twice
for her and the lad.

Once was Christmas. They had this preacher,
all the whores knew him to screw him;
he snuck up the back stairs, liked to
wear pink lace panties and get whipped.
So there he was preachin' sin and hellfire
and I busted out laughin' at that swelled up liar,
picturin' the poor bastard in panties. The choir
all stood up mad as hell, hollerin' at me

to shut up, this was the Lord's house, pointed
their fingers at her, said Shame. The anointed
'bout made me come unjointed, but then
the preacher calls her a sinful, fallen woman right
in front of the lad, and that's when I poked him, busted
his nose and lip, ripped his clothes, broke my knuckle.

She never took me again. Liars gives off a smell,
like a whore coverin' up a hard night with perfume;
I got nothin' against the Lord, but
If a silk-pantied whippin' boy is all he can afford

to come up with, I'll take the devil and his evil ways every time. I know I'm goin' to hell, but I'll be glad to get away from the righteous; most people's only religious from the waist up anyways.

The Indian Killer's Father

Will you talk about your father? he is asked.
Once Maw died me and him barely spoke.
But I'll tell ya this.
I had this mongrel dog, name of Butch.
He had a sideways kinda gait from where
a bull he was messin' with stove up his backsides.
He wasn't scareda nothin', ole Butch.
He slept with me, followed me everywhere,
we wasn't never apart for long. One time
I rode over to the next farm to help out
with the harvest. When I come home, first thing
I hollered for Butch.   Nothin'.
I went and asked the Old Man where he was.
Shot him, was all he said, cold.
I sat down like it was me been shot.
Why? I got out 'fore I went to chokin'.
He got after the rooster, the Old Man says.
I went to the barn fer my huntin' rifle,
thumbed 2 rounds in the chamber,
come for him.
He seen me comin', knew,
stands there on the porch waitin'.
Go 'head and shoot me. They'll hang you
'fore mornin', he says. I reckoned he was right.
Too much evidence. I put down the rifle.
That night I got some lamp oil,
soaked the porch real good, set the house on fire.
Can't prove nothin' with a fire.
Did he get out? he is asked.

Don't know. Saddled up, rode off fer good,
never looked back. Don't matter what ya save
from a burnin' house, it's what ya lose
that has the meanin'.
Butch, I said as I rode off.
The night was lit up like Sunrise.

The Indian Killer: Rules of Engagement

It was war, you done what you had to do.
But the Apaches was different,
they caught one of our patrols in a ravine,
surrounded 'em, took every one captive.
If they'da shot 'em, we cd take that, but
that's not what the Apaches done. No.

They staked 'em down, cut out their tongues,
burned out their eyes, then
turned 'em loose wanderin' in the hills.
When we found 'em, 3 was still alive but
nobody was glad they'd lived. They
was lost in the head, gone, everything just

rattling around loose and ruined so
we shot 'em. It was a kindness.
We found their camp near the Mexican border.
Right at dawn we rode in hard, torched
the lodges, shot the braves; cut and stabbed
the women; shot some, left mosta the babies

for the wolves. Somethin' broke in us then and
once it breaks, you can't get it back.
It wasn't no war then, it was meanness
and evil and hurt. Wasn't none of us
ever any good again.
Once you done somethin' like that,

ya can't go home no more,
ya jest wait on it to come for ya.
We was nursin' a hard grievance;
good men in a bad dream.

The Indian Killer Addresses the Question of Honor

They set me on 2 Army Surrender Commissions,
me and the generals and senators. They all knew me.
They brought in the defeated Chiefs and they
each laid down their rifles on the long table, but
not Sitting Bull. He laid down an Eagle feather and
all the suits and uniforms said, *What the hell?*
Ya can't recognize what ya ain't got, nor
lose what ya never had, but I knew what it meant;
it was honor, he was sayin'
It is over, finished, we are done like the Buffalo.
So I picked up that feather, took the gold medal
they give me in Washington, give it to him and
we looked at each other in the eye and nodded.
We knew who we was.

What he done was hold onta his honor, the one thing
we cdn't take from 'em. I seen it and I seen the cost
of what I'd lost, so I took the feather and I still got it.
A man holds onto any scrap of honor he's got left,
even if it's only a nickel's worth.
Honor's what we pay with,
to git by, git through, git along, survive, 'til
there ain't a nickel's worth left.
Then yr used up, spent, short-changed, not even
a penny's worth to make change fer a nickel.

Empires is built a nickel at a time, nickel
and dime the natives off the land, but the first

crime is killin' off all them that's gotta nickel's worth of honor; they're the prime targets, the first ta go. Nations is built on the lowest common denomination.

The Indian Killer Explains Sharpshooting

I'll tell ya how good I was.
Once the Army sent me out alone to pick off
an Injun raiding party that was raisin' hell
in Sioux country. I got on top of a boulder
in a draw, rifle barrel, face, hands, all
ashed over so wdn't nothin' give me away, then
I laid there for hours, not movin' a muscle,
flies crawlin' up my nose. Pretty soon
a big mean Rattler crawls up on the rock
in the hot Sun right next to my leg.
Now if I fire, the snake will spook
and bite me.

He stops there, doesn't go on.
But what happened? he is asked.

Right there you miss the point, he growls,
'cuz ya wanna know too much, have
all the answers wrote down there
in yr little damn book. Life don't work like that.
Point is, ya do whatever it takes, go through
whatever sufferin', to get yr shot.
There's a sweetness in that, a Grace.
That's the only Grace there is,
preparin' yr best shot.
Hit or miss don't matter.
Live or die don't matter. He jabs his finger.
If you ain't willin' to die

to take yr best shot, then
ya got no bizness on top of the boulder.

The Indian Killer's Discourse on Art

What did you learn from being a sharpshooter?
he is asked. It ain't enough bein' a good shot,
he said. Lots'a them didn't make it;
ya gotta master the body; like it er not,

don't matter, ya gotta be able to lay hid fer
hours at a time, flies crawlin' yr face,
and not move, not make a sound or you'll
blow yr cover and they'll kill ya without a trace.

Plan one shot ahead and keep movin' after
ya shoot, never nest in a tree er other place
with no exit, er they'll blow ya away.
Lots of 'em got took out that way, too tight a space.

Last thing, the thing that got most'a
the rest was, don't try fer the bull's eye,
don't go fer the head shot, the odds
of a miss is too high;

go fer the largest target, aim fer the body,
bring 'em down, disable 'em, take 'em outta play
real quick, 'fore they kin find ya
and return fire. Then ya kin lay

there at yr leisure and
pick 'em off, one
by one by
one.

The Indian Killer Joins Up with Cody

I wuz nearbout 60 when I headed east by train
to join up with Cody's Wild West Show.
Had you ever been on a train before? he is asked.
Hell, he laughs. Once I made 100 bucks in a day
shootin' Buffalo from a train, 100 hides.
That's how big the herds was.
So this Cody Show was cheap drunk's change but
It beat the Army, twenty-five bucks
a month fer a sharpshooter like me, 15 fer
reg'lars, that's all we got. Cody paid 60.

Did you know Buffalo Bill? he is asked.
Sometimes I called him Cody.
His one good eye fires up.
He's a goddam liar.
I killed a hundred Buffalo in one day, but
he told the papers it was him and
so that's how he got that name.
I cd outshoot any of 'em.
He got Sitting Bull for 100 but
only 60 fer me who shot Sitting Bull's horse

right out from under him and then
pumped 4 rounds into Sitting Bull but
he wouldn't go down.
Goddamdest thing I ever did see.
I guess maybe he's worth a hundred.
If I'da shot him, it'd be me

gittin' the hundred, not him.
I killed plenty jest like him, but
the last Injun fighter don't pay near as good
as the last Injun.

The Indian Killer Meets the President

We done the Cody Show at the White House once,
he relates. I come prancin' out on a white horse
shootin' blanks at a buncha Rez Injuns and
they proceeded to fall off their ponies like they
was shot; they gotta extra 2-bits if they fell off, so

4 wd fall off every time I shot. Then Sitting Bull
comes out and we act out the whole damned thing
all over again: I shoot a blank at his trick pony and
it falls down like it was shot, then
I fire off 4 blanks real quick

at Sitting Bull and it don't bother him,
he swats at 'em like he was swattin' away
goddam flies; that's how he done it
the first real time too,
goddamdest thing I ever did see, but

now it ain't worth a hundred bucks.
He runs off and they're clappin' and hollerin'.
Then we all line up to meet the President and
Missus President. She smells like a bar whore only
twice as ugly, wdn't of made a dime whorin' and

he shakes hands like a damn choir girl, never once
looked me in the good eye. I tell ya I didn't care fer him:
liars gives off a smell, like a dog
that's rolled in shit; he stunk.
I'd respect an Injun 'fore a politician;

an Injun'll kill ya if he has to but
a politician cuz he can.

The Indian Killer and Sitting Bull

Did you know Sitting Bull? he is asked.
First we fought each other, then
we done the Cody show together. Turns out
he liked a drink so I'd bring a bottle and
me and him wd laugh and tell stories.
I asked him once how he done it, swattin'
bullets away when I fired point blank at him.
He laughed so hard he like to bust his britches.
Magic, he says. Wdn't say no more.
He wasn't like the rest of 'em.

I liked Sitting Bull. Respected him.
He didn't care if he died.
He'd ride right up on you, bullets flyin'
just to touch you with his Coup stick. Dyin'
scared the hell out of the Army boys but
once she died I knew how it was.
I didn't care if I died, didn't scare me none.
Wd be glad ta die. But Bull
cd See what was in yr heart, wd tell me
things nobody but me and her knew.

He wasn't like the rest of 'em.
He had a power, maybe the devil's power,
but he never boasted even when he was
drunk as a lame Coyote. Nosir, he was
tough but quiet. Once he said, You kill
Indian, I kill white; all even. Warrior brothers.
He called me Shoots Straight.

I cdn't help it, I liked him,
even if he was an Injun.
We'd drink 'til the bottle was empty.

Another dead soldier, he'd say.
Another dead Injun, I'd say and
we'd laugh and pound each other on the back.
You'll say I'm crazy, but I liked him more
than any other man I ever knew. Fact
is he'll burn in hell with me and the whore.
I seen the Christians, don't take no shine
to them and their heaven. You can't beat
a bottle and the whore rubbin' my feet.
Me and the devil will get along jest fine.

You don't believe in God then? he is asked.
Only God cd'a made whores, he smiles.
He may live in Heaven, but he'll walk 100 miles
and sneak up the back stairs of hell
just like his preachers, just to get a smell
of a good whore. Then me and Him and Bull will
have a drink and a good laugh, tell stories
about the glories of women. I know God likes a drink;
I don't think you can fuck up the world this bad
sober.

The Indian Killer in Old Age

How old are you now Sir? he is asked.
99, he growls, don't give a damn
if I ever see a hundred. And
stop callin' me sir, this ain't
the goddam Army. No man shd fear
death, he continues, but every man shd fear
old age; it tempts ya to lie down and quit.
Death'll steal everything you got quick, but
old age takes a nickel at a time.

But doesn't wisdom come with old age?
he is asked. He laughs out loud,
part growl, part howl.
Most old men are damn fools, he drools, snot
drips down his lip; he wipes it on his sleeve.
Don't believe what you hear. I'm near blind,
piss my pants, can't eat right, night sweats.
Kiss my ass, I can barely walk, don't talk to me
about wise. Old age'll wise ya up alright.

Ya see then that nothin' lasts and
you ain't nothin' besides. It don't mean
a damn thing, none of it. A wise man
don't try ta make it mean somethin',
it just happens and you wait
fer one good shot, ya git yr shot
lined up and ya squeeze one off.
Old age, yr outta ammo so you sit here
old and cold,

waitin' ta git picked off.

Dirge:
Old Age Requires the Greatest Courage

Old Age Requires the Greatest Courage

The greatest courage is not needed for war,
but for ordinary people growing old.
Like soldiers, the aged are never very far
from death: many are called,
all are chosen. A soldier faces danger
then retreats, but for the old, going back
is not possible; they may hunger
for youth but pray for the luck
of a quick death. When one by one
the body's systems fail, they must be brave
and face annihilation of the flesh and bone,
the Soul clinging like a shipwrecked sailor, to love;
finally, love is all we are given
to navigate between exhaustion and heaven.

The Indian Killer Speaks of Love

You loved the whore didn't you? he is asked.
Her name was Elizabeth Joyce. You don't
call her a whore Miss, young as you are you
shd learn somethin' about respect. I kin call her
a whore but that's ta ease the hurt, nothin' else.
Don't talk to me about love. Lizbeth
was the only thing close to it I ever seen and
I cdn't do right by it, it was way more
than I cd handle. Sure, I come back to it
over and over, the way a wolf'll come back

to a water hole. Lizbeth cd love,
I seen that, but it hurt me a lot more
than it ever helped me. Love'll hurt you,
it'll break you more than any man
with a gun or fist. It'll make you want to
die, he said, and his good eye got narrow
and a fire was in it. Beware the sweet;
ya get used to it and the bitter arrow
follows, splits yr heart, leaves ya bleedin' in the street.
There's somethin' bigger'n love here; It'll beat

ya down, It don't pity them's in pain;
It's cold, It eats and swallows, It takes
good & bad, love & hate, it's all the same.
It don't give a damn, It just breaks
every goddam thing. It eats everything It makes.
Love ain't fer the weak,

only the strong kin bear the hurt.
The Gospels says it's the meek
inherits the Earth;
they kin have it fer all it's worth.

The Indian Killer Talks About Death

So you don't fear dying? he is asked.
Shit, you might just as well be scared
of the Sun risin', he hacks and spits, wipes.
It's everywhere. If a bullet don't get you
then old age will; I'da ruther a bullet,
but that's not how my deck was cut.
Bullet's easy, old age is mean and nasty.
Good nor bad don't matter a damn ta Death.
I seen the good suffer and that little
chicken-shit liar Cody got away scot-free.

Death's like a hungry Crow scourin' the land,
lookin' for somethin' to eat, devourin' everything,
always hungry, never satisfied, always lookin'.
A Crow don't care what it is or where
it's been, he'll eat it.
They was a tribe'a Crow Injuns,
horse thiefs.
That's what Death is, a thief.
It'll take everything you own right out
from under yr nose and can't you
nor nobody stop it. They's some
call me a killer, but way I see it,
Death is the killer, I'm just in His service.

If not me, Death'll find another boy,
there's always someone lookin' to serve.
We don't own nothin',

Death owns us.
Death'll say to yr face
what no man wd dare ta speak;

him that owns don't worry
'bout them that rents.

The Indian Killer's Vision

I was in the Black Hills, summer, hot
as a cheap gun barrel after a massacre.
Hell, I ain't gonna tell this; you'll think
I was crazy or dreamin' and maybe I was,
both at once. The heat'll do that to ya.

No, no. Please go on. I want to hear this,
he is urged. His good eye bores into you like
hot lead in tender flesh.
He is weighing, measuring.
I was stalkin' Crazy Horse, crafty

as a damn Coyote, almost never got a look
at him, never mind gettin' a good shot.
But that's the kinda work I done. So
I was layin' in the shade of a boulder when
I musta dozed off and started dreamin' 'cuz

next thing I know a Black Bear come up on me
big as a horse, biggest Bear I ever saw and
jest like in a dream I cdn't move, cdn't
lift my rifle to shoot. But this here is where
it gits crazy: he jest sat there starin' at me,

eatin' me alive with his eyes. I was par'lyzed,
not with fear, I wadn't afraid. That's why
I think it was a dream. Next thing I know,
he's gone like that and I cd see my body
scattered all around the boulder in pieces.

A ghost steps out, starts puttin' me
back together again. That's all they was to it.
What do you think it means? he is asked.
Don't mean sheeit, he snorts. The Injuns
they had somethin' we're missin'.

Don't know what it was,
cdn't never find it, didn't know
where to look nor what to look fer.
Jest drifted, torn up, put back together
with somethin' missin'.

I seen God up close, Miss;
It ain't what we think.
But white folks hafta know,
we can't live with a question, 'cuz
a question leaves ya lonely on yr deathbed.

The Indian Killer on His Deathbed

The encroaching darkness holds a hideous wisdom:
too late the shame, too late the remorse, too late
the heart burst open like a baby head-shot
in its mother's arms;
they are all there, every one of them with
their wounds open and bleeding, crowded
into the tiny rented room, spilling out into the hall,
sucking all the air out of the room and
out of him.

He gasps and struggles in the strangling dim,
clawing for a breath.
Some want to set him on fire, others
want to hang him.
Sitting Bull is standing there quietly.
Cody's offering 100 bucks to the one who
puts a bullet in his good eye.
At last, he thinks, the sonofabitch thinks
I'm worth a hundred,
Sitting Bull gets nothing.

Sitting Bull steps forward and the room
gets quiet.
You are responsible now for every one of these,
he says.
However many lifetimes it takes, now
you must work to provide for each of them.

He tries to raise his head to protest, but
it's no good.
So that's how the damn thing works,
he thinks. Why don't they tell you that

to begin with? Then he is alone
except for Sitting Bull.
Are you the devil or what? he gasps.
No, the devil didn't want you,
Sitting Bull smiles. *I'm nothing
but what you make me out to be. You
are stuck in this world until you pay.*
Then there is the unspeakable silence
and the burst-heart fails. He flails
once and no breath follows, only
the endless dirt road; everyone is
standing there waiting for him, silent,
watching.

He takes the first step, ready to go to work,
carrying the wound by himself,
thinking: There's no end to it;
I always thought there was an end.

Cody's Version of the Indian Killer

I did not like him much.
He had no respect.
He liked to call me Buffalo Bullshit
in front of the others, to the press.

I fired him 5 different times,
always took him back.
He was famous, you know but
he didn't know it; he couldn't read.

That was the good thing, meant I could
hire him cheap. They wrote these
dime novels about him: Jake Weston,
Indian Killer. So I had to have him

In the show. Crowds came to see him and
Sitting Bull do their fight.
Presidents wanted to meet them.
There was something about Jake Weston

that interested me. Oh he was
rough cut, hard drinker, coarse but
he was not a brute like so many of them.
He understood something more. I know,

I know, he claimed I lied about the Buffalo,
stole his thunder. *Is that true?* he is asked.
Maybe not, he says and stands up, walks away.
He turns. Elizabeth Joyce is what made him,

he says. She changed him. I think
he was more Indian than white man.
He went over.
Elizabeth was ½ Indian; he would

never tell you that, would he? He was
ashamed of it, took it out on the boy.
It's true I wanted to kill him sometimes,
he had no gratitude, but he had somethin',

I don't know what, it could be suffering,
that made him different. It almost made him noble.
He called the President a goddamn liar to his face
for what he done to the Indians. You should have

seen the President's face, looked like someone
had dipped him in dogshit and set him on fire.
No, I didn't like him but
you had to like him for that.

Sitting Bull Sees the Indian Killer

Shoots-Straight good bad man.
2 Spirits in him, make hard war,
make him sad good bad man,
make him carry big wound like

wound he give many others only
this don't kill, don't heal.
Me, Shoots-Straight, Warrior Brothers,
understand how it is inside.

He had the Power,
never knew it, couldn't kill him.
Many Warriors shoot, try to kill him
in the battles, never could;

he had the Power, just like me but
don't know, stayed little inside.
He told the truth, shoots straight.
Best shooter in soldier-army, way best,

could shoot grasshopper out of air,
this I saw with these eyes, twice
so no lucky.
Love Lakota woman, handsome woman, this

hurt him, confuse him, make him good man.
He don't know this. Thought like bad man,
act like good. Good win. He
don't know this; Power hidden from him,

keep him small inside. Power stay hidden
from man with 2 spirits in him.
Man with one Spirit hard to find;
Power find him.

Elizabeth Joyce's Last Will & Testimony

Oh, he could fool you because he was
tough, hard bark, big growl, sharp tooth,
bad deeds, but something was unbroken in him
that gets broken in most men.

You might call it courage, even honor. He told
the truth. *You loved him*, she is not asked, but
stated as fact. Her dark eyes grow luminous,
the way the Moon is on a clear night.

I was Moon Woman to my Mother, who was
Lakota Sioux, so it was hard for Jacob
to accept what I felt for him, but
he did the best he could. It was

more than love, Miss. It was where the ponies
go in summer, in the sweetgrass canyon
where there's a water hole and shade.
Was it joy? she is asked. She smiles

deeply. That's my name, Joyce: Elizabeth
Joyce Moon Woman. The nature of the Moon
Is to reflect the Light from the Sun.
My Mother saw my nature.

It was more than love. He was more than
just a good man. I was a Woman of Pleasure;

he understood that. He never faulted me
for what I was. Never. He couldn't do that
for himself. He didn't' tell you how
he supported us so I could stop working,
did he? He wouldn't.
Or how he helped Sitting Bull and the others

when they went back to the Prison Land?
He wouldn't. Or how he helped my sisters and
my Mother, or how he wept when our boy
went to jail? Oh no, he wouldn't tell you that.

It was more than love, Miss. It was
what can't be named. Some things
if you name them, they are diminished.
We name everything but understand nothing.

I am the Moon who shines in the Light
of what can't be named. That goes for him too;
better to say too little and
risk being misunderstood, than to say

too much and have everyone think they know.

President Franklin Pierce Is Questioned

*President Pierce, you were President when
Buffalo Bill brought his show to the White House?*
Oh yes, it was a wonderful event.

Cody was a great man, a real entertainer.
We were glad to have them there.
Mrs. Pierce and Mrs. Cody were friendly, you know.

You met Jake Weston then? he is asked.
His eyes narrow.
His nostrils flare.

He sits up straight.
His knuckles whiten on the arms of the chair.
He was a liar, a drunkard, a thief and

a whore chaser, he finally spits out
between clenched teeth.
He was an evil man,

a disgrace and
I told Cody so. He said
he would fire him and I believe he did.

Now let's not talk about unpleasant things, Miss.
Let's talk about Buffalo Bill Cody. He was
a great American, a great man,

killed 100 Buffalo in a single day, you know.

The Preacher's Sworn Statement

He is a God—, —a filthy liar, full
of corruption, a sinner, a truly evil man,
spawn of the Devil Himself.
God only knows how many lives
are on his immortal Soul, how much blood
is on his hands. He was

as evil as any man I ever met.
If you want to take the word
of a man like that, God Bless you, Miss.
The kind of filthy evil lies he told you
are exactly what I would expect from
a man like that. Exactly.

If you want the truth, talk to my wife,
ask the good people of this town,
they'll tell you the truth.
Look who he stayed with, a prostitute
from the Silver Dollar, that right there
should tell you all you need to know

about the kind of man he was.
May his Soul burn in hell forever.
We all get exactly what we deserve,
as God is my witness.
Sin has a smell about it, like sulfur.
Jake Weston stank of sin, he was
an abomination in the sight of the Lord,
a putrefaction in the noseholes of Jehovah.
Never ask me again about the panties, Miss.

The Indian Killer on Being Human

What do you think of Humanity? he is asked.

An immeasurable fear,
an old sadness,
half already dead, the other
half dyin' brightness
like the Moon,
I've seen it
sinking into the water,
dissolvin' like flesh
too delicate to persevere.
One morning is all we're given,
one glimpse, one look at the trees,
one sip of water, one touch
of a woman's lips, just once
layin' on a boulder in the Sun.

There's somethin' in us that's equal
to everything, it's too big
to speak of, it's all shining,
I've seen it; then
there's somethin' hard and ugly,
mean and scared, can't stand
its sadness so it goes everywhere
lookin' fer somethin' to hurt.
I've seen it too.

I've heard there's some made these
2 things get along peaceful, but

I never figgered how ya cd. do that,
the sadness just ate up
the light in me.
How can you pray? Who
you gonna pray to?
Who's prayin' and fer what?
We fell from somewhere into somethin'
like a bird fallin' in a still lake,
then we srirred it all up,
raised the mud offa the bottom.

Wadn't no peace ever again.

Requiem:
The Indian Killer Explains Manifest Destiny

The Indian Killer Explains Manifest Destiny

Why did you kill the Indians? he is asked.
Becuz they was there.
It had to be done.
They was in the way.
They wouldn't give it up.

Give what up?
The fight.
Their ways.
They didn't believe in God.
They had the land.
They wouldn't give it up.
So we took it.

Why?
Becuz we could.
Becuz we believed back then we was good.
Becuz there had to be blood.
You take a man who resists and brings
doubt into what's agreed and understood,
you nail him to a piece of wood.
That settles things.
It should.
That's the end of the story;
without blood, no glory.

You don't add up the honest score, the cost
to them that's won or them that's lost.
Them that's won is left alone
without excuse;
they refuse
to atone.

Postlude:
Man and His Machines

Man and His Machines

Across the street in the boneyard
I see a man with a backhoe digging a grave
that he once dug by hand in 4-5 hours; now
he is done in 20 minutes and he isn't tired,
his hands aren't calloused, he no longer works
with his body, he doesn't get dirty.

It is when a man works with a machine,
works beyond what his body alone could do,
that he becomes dangerous; now he is able
to bring mountains down and change the course
of rivers, to level whole forests and fish
the oceans until they have nothing left to give.

When a man had only his body to work with
he knew his limits and his place, he knew
what time was by the seasons. But
give a man a machine and now he needs
Conscience and humility or else he will
do more harm than good; he will behave

recklessly, smitten by a false sense of power
because he can fell a mighty Cedar in less than an hour.
With machine comes a greater responsibility;
now a man must act from his inherent nobility,
from a sense that all things have dignity and Grace,
or beauty disappears from the world without a trace.

Permissions

"You and I Are Planting" and "The Buffalo Dance" first appeared in *The Comstock Review*.

An earlier version of "Big Soldier Explains Why He Will Not Surrender" first appeared in *The Canary River Review*.

An earlier version of "Words Are Not Actions" and "The Sioux Dog Dance" first appeared in *The New York Quarterly*.

An earlier version of "The Battle Axe" first appeared in *The Way of Power*.

"The Law of the Land" won the 2nd prize in the Jewish Currents poetry competition and was published in *World to Come* anthology. It was reprinted in *LILIPOH* magazine.

"The Indian Killer Explains Manifest Destiny" first appeared in *Rattle*.

"The Horses of War" first appeared in *Cross Currents*.

"Old Age Requires the Greatest Courage" first appeared in *Rattle* and was a finalist for the Rattle Poetry Prize.

RED HAWK was the Hodder Fellow in the Humanities at Princeton University in 1991–92, and is currently a professor at the University of Arkansas at Monticello. He is an award-winning author of eight poetry collections and two nonfiction spiritual self-help books. His poems have also appeared in *The Atlantic, Kenyon Review, Poetry, Atlanta Review, Shenandoah, Tampa Review,* and many others.

He has two terrific daughters and three splendid grandsons, and lives in Monticello, Arkansas with his sweetheart Chandrika.

www.ingramcontent.com/pod-product-compliance
Lightning Source LLC
Chambersburg PA
CBHW050600300426
44112CB00013B/2003